Art Nouveau Patterns I

ILLUSTRATIONS BY JULIANNA KUNSTLER

ART *of* COLORING®

www.juliannakunstler.com

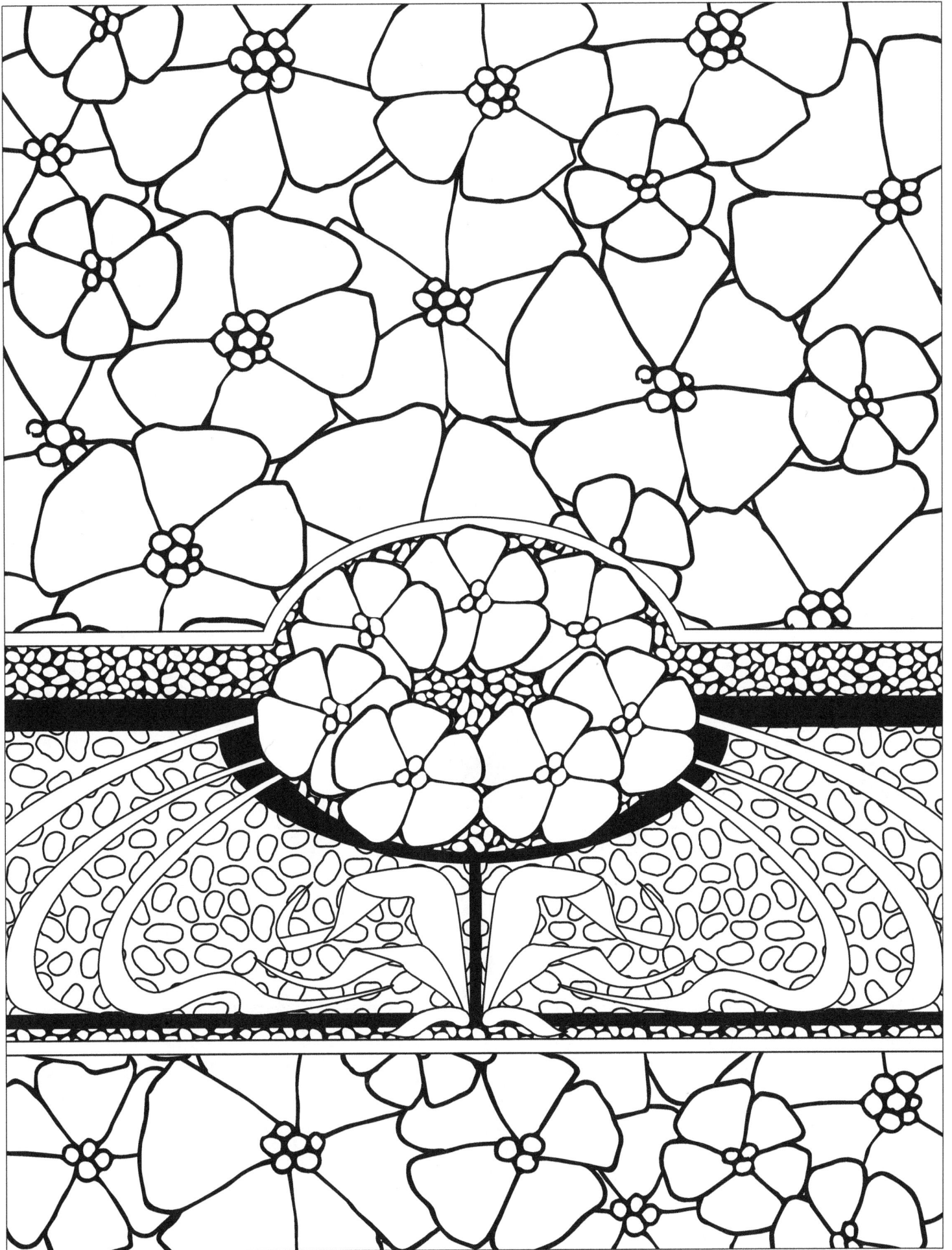

© julianna kunstler

©julianna kunstler

© julianna kunstler

© julianna kunstler

©julianna kunstler

©Julianna Kunstler

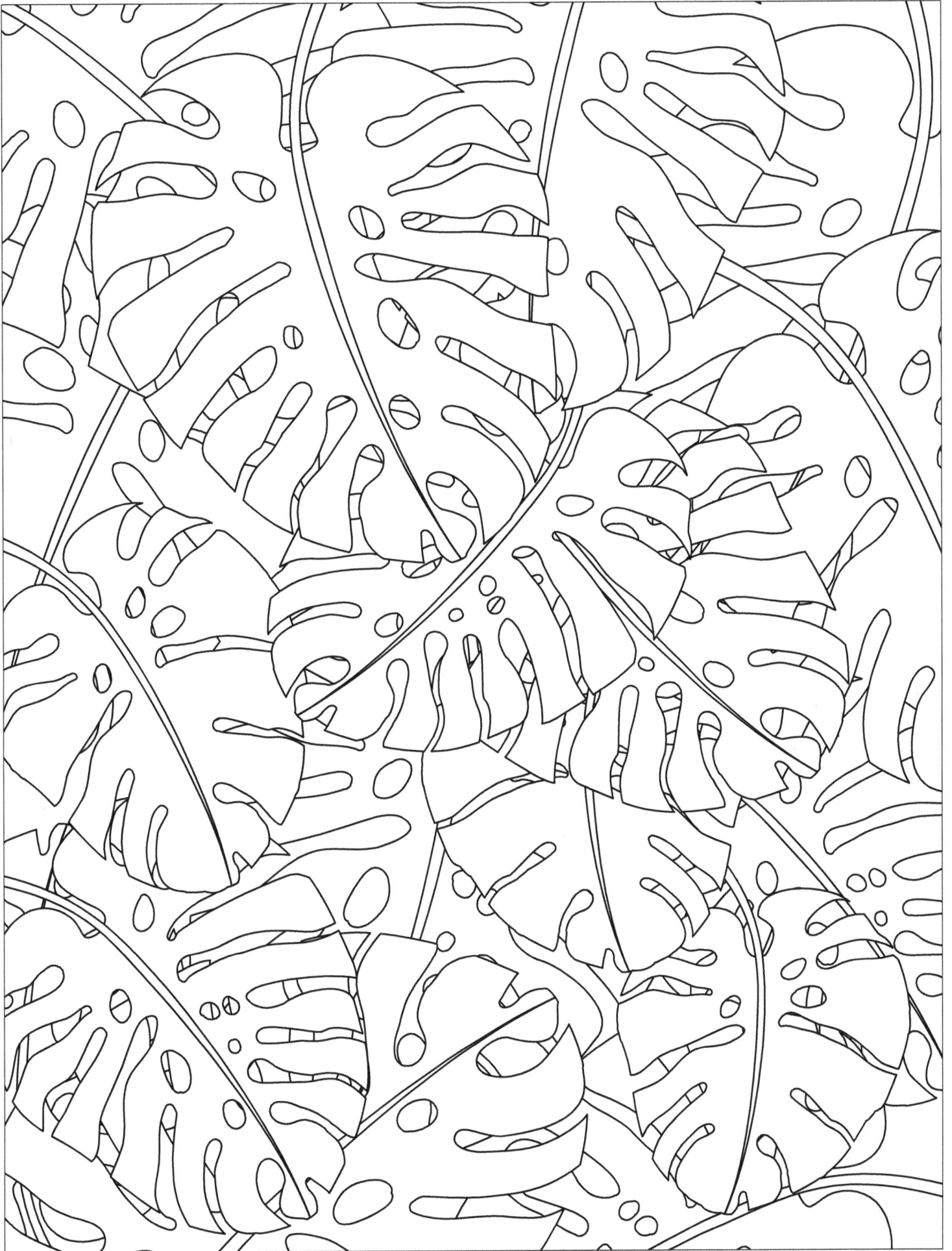

©julianna kunstler

©julianna kunstler

www.ingramcontent.com/pod-product-compliance
Lightning Source LLC
Chambersburg PA
CBHW081341090426

42737CB00017B/3246